INSPIRATION F

C000161976

GET
FIRED UP!

Are You Ready To Start Taking Massive Action?

Paul Patton

Table of Contents

Chapter 1:

Five Inspiration Pillars For Men

The Traditional Man

Much has been said (and written too) about the traditional man. But, who really is he? The traditional man is the same as the modern man except that he was what society viewed masculinity at the time.

Men were known to be ruthlessly fierce with zero emotions. Their hearts solely performed the blood circulation function, nothing more. Actually, nobody knew how it felt to be a man except for men themselves. They hardly ever talked about it, so the guesswork continued.

The modern man has inherited the software of his predecessor and he is programmed in the same way. The advent of women empowerment was initially opposed by male chauvinists but they later bowed down. This is the reason why the gospel of feminism is not new to the ears of every lady out there.

The Road To Manhood Is Muddy And Swampy

After the empowerment of the female gender (which they rightfully deserved after being 'ruled' by men), the modern man was not taught how to handle the empowered woman.

It has been a push and pull lifestyle – instead of a complementary one – and this has not been any easier for Adam's gender.

However, men are still men. Where do they get the inspiration to wake up daily and chase their dreams? In the UK, the BBC in 2019 reported that domestic violence abuse against men has been on the rise and many more men are suffering in silence.

Pillars of inspiration.

Despite all the difficulties, for hard times make a man, five pillars are of great inspiration to men. Here they are:

1. Physical Strength

Men are proud of their masculine energy. They even brag about it! Their swiftness and agility in response are unmatched. Yes, there are physically fit ladies and it is a good thing. Men, however, take pride in it more.

From an early age, boys are raised up to go out on the field and play with their peers. They are also called upon to help with manual tasks. This discipline instilled in them is a source of inspiration to keep living their best life because the world needs them.

2. Source Of Income

This debate has never been settled – men are the traditional providers in families. In this era, roles are quickly changing and we have ladies too heading companies or working in different capacities to also fend for their families.

However, the pride of a man is his work. Regardless of how meager or plentiful they earn; men find pride in working for a living. Nothing is satisfying for a man like going back home with a day's wages or a monthly salary every month end. It makes him feel 'in charge'.

Work inspires men to live each day at a time even when work conditions are unfavorable.

3. The Traditional Leadership Advantage

Even with a changing society, families still look up to fathers for leadership. This does not make mothers any inferior. They still complement their husbands in making family decisions and that is beautiful.

Men are inspired to be better today than they were yesterday. They are an inspiration to younger males and would not want to let them down. This motivates them in their lives that they are still useful for they are expected to provide leadership.

4. Family

Families are the reason why men get out of bed daily for work. Most men are breadwinners in their families.

If not for themselves, men are inspired by their families. Their wives and children are the motivation they need to live each day at a time.

5. Fellow Tribe Of Men

Iron sharpens iron, so is a responsible man molded by another. Other successful men inspire men to work hard each day and be successful like them.

It is some kind of a brotherhood that a man cannot fail his brother. This inspiration makes them wield tough situations of life just to make it in the end.

Here is what they did not tell you: being a man is difficult and at the same time, the easiest thing if you have the right motivation.

Chapter 2:

Five Ways To Share Your Gifts With The World

Behold, You Are Gifted!

Yes, you are gifted. We all are in one way or the other. Well, for starters, a gift is something special that you are given as a reward for doing something good. Some people believe it comes from the gods, others say it is from nature while a handful of others cannot really explain its origin.

The bottom line is that you are gifted and you are meant to serve the world with it. It could be yours but still meant for the service of other people. The idea is that everyone should universally be able to benefit from the gifts poured onto the sons of men.

One thing about gifts that most people miss is that there is no competition on who has the best gift. They are meant to complement each other. Together, our gifts can elevate us to higher positions. The world can be ours to rule if only we bring our gifts together and put our pride aside.

In case you are wondering what gifts we are talking about, here is a whole list of them: making handwork artifacts, singing, dancing, inspirational talk, writing, acting, and many more in the list.

Do not keep your gifts to yourself, share them with the world as it was intended. Here is how :

1. Do Free Blogs and Vlogs.

There are tens if not hundreds of free sites where you can start your blog. All you need to have is a determined mind to do it. No excuse can stand in your way as long as you are willing. Many people have done it and many more continue to launch their blogs daily.

Identify what it is you want to share with the world then take that bold step today. Many people globally in their millions lack the gift that you have been blessed with. You owe them some little light; don't you think so?

But why should you do it for free? Do it for free because not everyone has the money to access paid information. They could even be using public Wi-Fi!

However, you can later on segment some premium content for sale. Even the readers who saw the free version will be motivated to buy your payable content.

2. Donate Your Free Time To Train

Understandably, time is a limited resource that we do not have in plenty. One of the best things you can do is to share your time to train other people who would want to become like you.

You might have reached the level you are in without any help. Do not let others struggle in the same way you did. Be generous with your gift and show them the light.

There are many online platforms you can use to reach even those in remote places. All you need is to make that decision today.

3. Share Your Resources

Not everybody is lucky to access the resources you have. They could be gifted like you are but cannot maximize their gifts because they lack the means.

Be kind to share your resources with the fellow gifted people you meet. Nature shall repay you one day for that. The more you share your resources, the more you equally grow to new heights. That is the mystery of nature.

4. Serve With Your Gifts

You were not gifted to be bossy or order other people around. You were gifted so that you can serve your community. Your gift is the answer to the problems of many others. Present them with a solution today.

You can serve by organizing other free performances together with other gifted people. One free entertainment performance could be your source of fame and the beginning of many more paid performances.

5. Mentor The Upcoming Generation

The least you can do to give back to society is to mentor the upcoming generation. You will have a great impact on their lives and they will forever be grateful to you for inspiring them to be great and make their gifts useful as you do.

Mentorship is hard to come by. When you change the life of one or two through mentorship, they will carry that gift to many more others.

There are many ways of sharing your gifts with the world but these are more pronounced. Pay attention to them.

Chapter 3:

Five Ways To Be Inspired

Inspiration

What really is inspiration? It is what pushes you to go the extra mile. Inspiration is what fuel is to a motor vehicle. It powers it to continue with the journey.

You are never late to be inspired. Every moment is a time for inspiration. At any one point in our lives, we need to be inspired to do more. Sometimes are demotivated by the outcomes of life when we do not get what we had hoped for. That is not the time to throw in the towel.

All you need to do is look in the right direction. You need a second voice to encourage you and pat you on the shoulder.

An inspired person is transformed and renewed in their thoughts. It is like they dropped from the skies because all they think of is how they shall beat that target or how they will turn around their fortunes.

Not many people in this generation are inspired to move towards their goals. Here are five ways to be inspired:

1. Reflect On Your Achievements

Your life could have reached a plateau phase, at least in your eyes. You may lack the motivation to move ahead with your plans because everything seems to be pre-determined. The good news is that a plateau is better than level ground.

Turn your head and look at the far that you have come from. You overcame what others did not. Now is not the time to give up.

Think of the promise you gave your loved ones and consider how far your hard work has brought you. Imagine the smiles and laughter on their faces when you finally make it.

That is the spirit! Keep pushing!

2. Focus On Your Goals, Not Problems

The end goal of your journey is what you should focus on, never on your problems.

Consider the example of a lion chasing its prey. When he chooses a particular antelope from a herd, there is no turning back. He will keep chasing it until he wins. It does not matter whether another animal will pass in front of him. He will not lose focus on the one he had selected.

Victory tastes sweet. You should not think about anything that will make you miss it. Nothing is worth missing the prize.

There is a reason why you set out on the path you have chosen. Stick to whatever inspired you in the first place.

3. Have A Mentor

Do you have someone whom you idolize? There is this person who is all you would want to be. You would give everything in exchange to be him/her. Their dressing, their work ethic, and all their personal lifestyle reflect your desires and ambitions.

Mentors are people who inspire you not to be average. Whenever you are at the brink of giving up, their level of success cannot give you peace.

Your inspiration shoots above the roof when you spend time with them. Use your time with them to learn about their journey and how they overcame the challenges they faced.

Most important is that the success and failures of your mentor will make you realize they are also human but they managed to overcome it all.

You too can make it!

4. Build Your Self-Confidence

The reason why some people are demotivated is because of low self-confidence. They do not believe in themselves. They hand their competitors any slight opportunity on a platter. They suffer from an inferiority complex.

Build your personality. Train, read, and research. Do what it takes to give you confidence in your ability. Do not be timid for any reason.

Do not be your own enemy. When experts are being called forward and you are one of them, proudly move forward. What you despise in you is the dream of many people out there.

5. Stay Updated

It is important to be up to date with the latest trends in your field of interest. Do not lag behind because you will not feel the need to catch up.

There is an inspiration to catch up with the latest developments. The more you follow closely, the more you want to keep up. This is enough motivation.

These five ways will inspire you to get out of your comfort zone. It is what you really need in the wake of stiff competition everywhere.

Chapter 4:

5 Inspiration Stories For Men

These 5 motivational stories will encourage you to follow your dreams, treat others with kindness, and never give up on yourself.

1. Laziness Won't Get You Anywhere

"In ancient times, a king had his men place a boulder on a roadway. He then hid in the bushes, and watched to see if anyone would move the boulder out of the way. Some of the king's wealthiest merchants and courtiers passed by and simply walked around it.

Many people blamed the King for not keeping the roads clear, but none of them did anything about getting the stone removed.

One day, a peasant came along carrying vegetables. Upon approaching the boulder, the peasant laid down his burden and tried to push the stone out of the way. After much pushing and straining, he finally managed.

After the peasant went back to pick up his vegetables, he noticed a purse lying in the road where the boulder had been. The purse contained many gold coins and note from the King explain that the gold was for the person who removed the boulder from the road."

2. Don't Say Something You Regret Out Of Anger

"There once was a little boy who had a very bad temper. His father decided to hand him a bag of nails and said that every time the boy lost his temper, he had to hammer a nail into the fence.

On the first day, the boy hammered 37 nails into that fence.

The boy gradually began to control his temper over the next few weeks, and the number of nails he was hammering into the fence slowly decreased. He discovered it was easier to control his temper than to hammer those nails into the fence.

Finally, the day came when the boy didn't lose his temper at all. He told his father the news and the father suggested that the boy should now pull out a nail every day he kept his temper under control.

The days passed and the young boy was finally able to tell his father that all the nails were gone. The father took his son by the hand and led him to the fence.

'You have done well, my son, but look at the holes in the fence. The fence will never be the same. When you say things in anger, they leave a scar just like this one. You can put a knife in a man and draw it out. It won't matter how many times you say I'm sorry, the wound is still there.'"

3. Stop Wasting Your Time Complaining

"People visit a wise man complaining about the same problems over and over again. One day, he decided to tell them a joke and they all roared with laughter.

After a few minutes, he told them the same joke and only a few of them smiled.

Then he told the same joke for a third time, but no one laughed or smiled anymore.

The wise man smiled and said: 'You can't laugh at the same joke over and over. So why are you always crying about the same problem?'"

4. Damaged Souls Still Have Worth

"A shop owner placed a sign above his door that said: 'Puppies For Sale.'

Signs like this always have a way of attracting young children, and to no surprise, a boy saw the sign and approached the owner; 'How much are you going to sell the puppies for?' he asked.

The store owner replied, 'Anywhere from $30 to $50.'

The little boy pulled out some change from his pocket. 'I have $2.37,' he said. 'Can I please look at them?'

The shop owner smiled and whistled. Out of the kennel came Lady, who ran down the aisle of his shop followed by five teeny, tiny balls of fur.

One puppy was lagging considerably behind. Immediately the little boy singled out the lagging, limping puppy and said, 'What's wrong with that little dog?'

The shop owner explained that the veterinarian had examined the little puppy and had discovered it didn't have a hip socket. It would always limp. It would always be lame.

The little boy became excited. 'That is the puppy that I want to buy.'

The shop owner said, 'No, you don't want to buy that little dog. If you really want him, I'll just give him to you.'

The little boy got quite upset. He looked straight into the store owner's eyes, pointing his finger, and said;

'I don't want you to give him to me. That little dog is worth every bit as much as all the other dogs and I'll pay full price. In fact, I'll give you $2.37 now, and 50 cents a month until I have him paid for.'

The shop owner countered, 'You really don't want to buy this little dog. He is never going to be able to run and jump and play with you like the other puppies.'

To his surprise, the little boy reached down and rolled up his pant leg to reveal a badly twisted, crippled left leg supported by a big metal brace. He looked up at the shop owner and softly replied, 'Well, I don't run so well myself, and the little puppy will need someone who understands!'"

5. Never Let One Failure From The Past Hold You Back In The Future

"As a man was passing the elephants, he suddenly stopped, confused by the fact that these huge creatures were being held by only a small rope tied to their front leg. No chains, no cages. It was obvious that the elephants could, at anytime, break away from their bonds but for some reason, they did not.

He saw a trainer nearby and asked why these animals just stood there and made no attempt to get away. 'Well,' trainer said, 'when they are very young and much smaller we use the same size rope to tie them and, at that age, it's enough to hold them. As they grow up, they are conditioned to believe they cannot break away. They believe the rope can still hold them, so they never try to break free.'

The man was amazed. These animals could at any time break free from their bonds but because they believed they couldn't, they were stuck right where they were."

Chapter 5:

6 Gut Feelings You Should Not Ignore

Do you have a voice within your head that tells you what's right and what's wrong? Do you ever know what you should do without knowing how you came to that conclusion? Some individuals refer to it as a gut feeling, while others refer to it as intuition, and still, others refer to it as a sixth sense. Whatever name you give it, there's no doubting the strength of human instinct. These unexpected, seemingly unexplained sentiments come over us when we need them the most, and you can count on them to guide you to the best decision possible in the heat of the moment. Our instincts are expressions of our subconscious ideas, and they assist us to understand ourselves and the world around us on a far deeper level. Many people, however, struggle to trust their instincts because they allow their worries, questions, and hesitations to clog their heads. They opt to listen to erroneous logic rather than their gut instincts, which can lead to unhappiness, dissatisfaction, and uncertainty later in life. With that in mind, here are some instincts you should never dismiss:

1. This Is Dangerous

Is the circumstance you're in now dangerous to you? Is your instinct telling you that trouble is on the way? Do you feel compelled to turn around or go the other way? Pay attention to how you're feeling. Your instincts can always tell you when you're in danger, saving you from several potentially disastrous situations. Maybe your inner voice is advising you not to do something or that you should avoid a certain person. When something horrible is about to happen, you can always feel it in your gut, so don't ignore it.

2. Other People Are In Danger

Your instincts can recognize when you're in danger, but they can also feel when other people are in danger and alert you to the situation. People can hide a lot beneath their outward appearances, even if it doesn't appear so on the surface. Listen to your gut instincts, and you might well save someone's life or keep them out of harm's way.

3. I'm Making A Mistake

Your subconscious may pick up on danger indications that you aren't aware of, so you should trust it when it warns you that something is wrong. This is usually a strong and unmistakable feeling of unease, intended to alert you that what you're doing isn't proper. Try not to reason with it or apply logic; if something doesn't feel right, don't do it. There's a reason you're feeling this way, even if you don't realize it yet. Your instincts are simply trying to keep you from making a mistake you'll come to regret.

4. I'm Not Feeling Well

People who have had a stroke or a traumatic brain injury frequently indicate that they knew something wasn't quite right with them minutes before the disaster (Kutschera & Ryan, 2009). So, if anything isn't right with your body, don't wait for it to worsen. Be alert to the symptoms that anything is wrong with you (physically, mentally, or emotionally), and don't discount your instincts when they tell you something is amiss.

5. Something's Wrong

More than immediate danger can be avoided using your intuition. It can also assist you in avoiding situations that may be detrimental to your mental and emotional health, such as a terrible relationship, an incompatible partner, or an unfulfilling career. If you feel weird most days, as if something is wrong but can't put your finger on it, your instincts are probably attempting to protect you from causing your misery. Don't just brush it off; get to the bottom of the issue and follow your intuition to the proper solution.

6. This Feels Right

Last but not least, when it comes to knowing what's best for you, you should always trust your intuition. Do you have a strong attraction to someone? Is there something you truly want to do regardless of the odds? This is your inner voice reassuring you that you are exactly where you should be. You're pleased and content because you know you're doing something right deep inside. You don't even have to think about it because it flows naturally. When you know, you know.

Conclusion

It goes without saying that when your gut is trying to tell you something, you should pay attention. Instincts are often unpredictable and mysterious, but you don't have to understand them to follow them. Allow yourself to be guided by your inner voice by clearing your mind, quieting your fears, and being guided by your inner voice. Everything else will fall into place once you follow your heart and trust your instincts.

Chapter 6:

6 Signs Your Mental Health is Getting Worse

If you typically have mild or intermittent depression symptoms, you might notice immediately if they suddenly become more severe or persistent. Still, the different types of depression can involve a range of symptoms, and changes might creep up slowly instead of falling on you all at once. You might not always recognize small but steady changes in your day-to-day mood until you suddenly feel a whole lot worse than you usually do.

If any of the following signs sound familiar, it's worth talking to your primary care doctor, therapist, or another healthcare professional about a new approach to treatment. If you haven't yet started treatment for depression, talking to a therapist about these symptoms is a good next step.

1. Almost Nothing Sparks Your Interest

Depression commonly involves a decrease in your energy levels and a loss of pleasure in your favourite hobbies and other things you usually enjoy. As you work toward recovery, you'll usually find your interest in these activities slowly begins to return, along with your energy.

2. With Worsening Depression, You Might Notice the Opposite

It may not just seem difficult to find the motivation for exercise, socializing, and other hobbies. Anhedonia, or difficulty experiencing joy and pleasure, is a core symptom of depression.

You might also have trouble mustering up enough energy to go to work or take care of basic responsibilities, like paying bills or preparing meals. Even necessary self-care, like showering and brushing your teeth, might feel beyond your current abilities.

3. You Spend More Time Alone

With depression, you might find it challenging to enjoy the company of others for a number of reasons. You may not feel up to socializing simply because you have less energy. Emotional numbness can make the social interactions you usually enjoy seem pointless.

Feelings of guilt, irritability, or worthlessness can also complicate your mood and make avoidance seem like the safer option. There's nothing wrong with spending time alone when you enjoy it. An increasing sense of loneliness, on the other hand, can make your mood even worse. You might begin to feel as if no one understands or cares about your experience.

4. Your Mood Gets Worse at Certain Times Of Day

Changes in how you experience symptoms might also suggest worsening depression. Your symptoms may have previously remained mostly stable throughout the day. Now, you notice they intensify in the morning or evening. Or perhaps they feel much worse on some days instead of remaining fairly consistent from day to day.

5. You Notice Changes in Eating And Sleeping Patterns

Depression often affects appetite and sleep habits. When it comes to appetite changes, you might find yourself eating more than usual. You could also lose your appetite entirely and feel as if you have to force yourself to eat.

Sleep changes often happen on a similar spectrum. You could have a hard time staying awake and feel exhausted enough to sleep all day — but you could also struggle to fall asleep or wake up often throughout the night. Trouble sleeping at night can mean you need to nap during the day to catch up, so you might end up drifting off at unusual times. This can affect your energy and concentration and further disrupt your sleep.

6. Intensifying Emotional Distress

If you have depression, you'll likely notice the following:

- hopelessness

- sadness

- a pessimistic outlook or catastrophic thinking

- feelings of guilt, shame, or worthlessness

- a sense of numbness

- problems with concentration or memory

- These feelings sometimes increase over time, so you might find yourself:

- fixating on negative thoughts

- worrying what others think of you or believing loved ones consider you a burden

- crying more often

- considering self-harm as a way to ease distress or numbness

- having frequent thoughts of suicide, even if you don't intend to act on them

If this distress persists or continues to get worse even with treatment, connect with a healthcare professional right away. It's not unusual for mental health symptoms to fluctuate over time. These changes may not always have a clear cause. Sometimes, though, they happen in response to specific triggers.

A few factors that could help explain worsening depression symptoms include:

- Stress
- Your treatment plan
- A different mental health condition
- Medication side effects
- Substance use

Chapter 7:

7 Signs You Are Emotionally and Mentally Exhausted

Riding the tumultuous rollercoaster known as life can be exhausting at times. You're high up one minute, and then you're back down where you started the next. When the lows outnumber the highs, though, the journey becomes boring. Instead, you'll be completely depleted on almost every level. Many people get intellectually and emotionally weary, resulting in many unpleasant symptoms. These symptoms may interfere with your daily routine, hurting productivity and relationships. If you see these indications, it's conceivable you're going through a difficult time in your life:

1. You Are Easily Irritated

You've been impacted by the tiniest of things recently. Negativity is everywhere around you, and it irritates you at any moment. You tend to lose your cool. As the days pass, you begin to lose hope. You become increasingly annoyed due to your ineptitude and lack of power. Unfortunately, this can lead to venting your frustrations on those closest to you, who don't necessarily deserve it.

2. You Always Feel Low and Lack Motivation in Your Life

You always get the feeling that something terrible will happen. You've lost hope in life, and nothing can persuade you to keep going. You believe you are unable to complete the task at hand. You're having trouble finding the motivation you require. Goals that once motivated you to work hard are no longer sufficient. This is especially tough to deal with at work or school when deadlines for various activities or assignments are looming. However, if you are not driven to complete those tasks, you will not complete them on time... and they will pile up, causing you to procrastinate even more. This could result in you failing classes or receiving work warnings. But if you're numb, you're not going to give a damn about that, are you?

3. You Experience Fits of Anxiety Quite Often

You are becoming increasingly stressed as a result of your exhaustion. Anxiety attacks are growing commonplace. You become overly concerned. You get anxious over the tiniest of things.

4. You Can't Sleep Properly

You frequently feel as if you are in the wrong place. The overwhelming sense of tiredness makes it difficult to quiet your mind and fall slumber. As a result, insomnia becomes another item on the to-do list. You are always exhausted, and all you want to do is sleep, yet you cannot do so. Why? Because your mind is racing, and you can't seem to break the cycle. Just as you begin to fall off, some anxiety will interrupt and jolt you awake, preventing you from getting that much-needed rest... compounding the exhaustion that is already draining you dry.

5. You Sense a Kind of Detachment

You no longer feel a connection to anyone or anything. Nothing has an impact on you. You are neither happy nor sad. It's as if you're just a body with no feelings. You've become deafening. Whatever you're dealing with has sapped your energy to the point that you can't experience the emotions you normally do when confronted with a scenario or subject. This is similar to depression; however, instead of being burdened by emotion, you're burdened by the lack of it.

6. You Cry for No Reason At All

If you've reached the stage when having toothpaste come from your toothbrush first thing in the morning causes you to burst out shouting... That is not acceptable. We lose the ability to cope with hard situations when we are physically and psychologically weary, and routine day-to-day stress is amplified. It's acceptable if you've found yourself sobbing in front of coworkers, friends, or even strangers.

7. You Feel Dizzy and Nauseous

Nausea and dizziness are indicators that you need to rest, and getting enough of it should be your top concern. These things occur due to your body's inability to cope with the stress and resulting in a breakdown. When a person has a mental breakdown, it is natural for them to become physically ill. This is especially true if you carry worry in your stomach or tighten your muscles instinctively to protect yourself from whatever is bothering you.

Conclusion

You can assist lessen the symptoms of emotional tiredness by making some lifestyle modifications. These tactics will be difficult to use at first, but they will get easier as you develop healthy habits. Small changes in your daily routine can help you manage your symptoms and avoid emotional fatigue. Once you've identified the symptoms of emotional weariness, work on eliminating them from your life.

Chapter 8:

Ten Ways To Become Mentally Stronger

Mental strength is a very great asset. Seek to grow it daily and you shall stand out from the crowd. There is one true test of knowing your mental strength. Seek to know the honest opinion of people whom you have interacted with. They can assess you better on how you responded to issues that required your attention. The good news is that there are tried, tested, and proven ways on how you can increase your mental strength. Here are ten ways:

1. Having Healthy Debates

Debates form an important part of growing your mental strength and social skills. There are two sides to every debate. Persuading your opponents that your position of the matter being discussed is the right way and not theirs is an uphill task. You cannot shout them down to submission or physically pull them over to your side. Listen to good debaters' debates and watch how they ask very important questions. Your mental strength grows as you engage like-minded people in critical thinking. It takes one sharp mind to strengthen another because iron sharpens iron.

2. Taking Interest in Mathematics and Science

All subjects are equally important. Mathematics and science just engage the mind a little bit more than others. These subjects involve a lot of logic and accurate analysis which is why they are fit to strengthen your mind. Start reading scientific theories that explain the difficult phenomenon. This will make you question what you considered normal. You will become mentally stronger with every analysis you make.

3. Learn To Accept Defeat

A mentally strong person knows that defeat is an important part of learning. It means you have not got it right but learned another way of how not to do things. Defeat will not break you down when you accept it as part of life. You emerge stronger every time people expect you to succumb to it.

4. Believe in Philosophy or Religion

Philosophy and religion hold very important pillars for society. They seek to explain what is a mystery to date. The creation and evolution stories are examples of theories developed to explain the origin of man. When you follow either of them, you will ask hard questions about particular beliefs that most people hold to date. This is your path to freedom of your mind!

5. Play Mind Games

Do you know that all work without play makes Jack a dull boy? An important part of the play is mind games. They include reverse psychology intending to get other people to reveal their true intentions.

Mind games help build a strong mind because you can penetrate the mind of another person through a simple conversation. You study their responses and attitude to life and you can choose whether or not to keep them as friends.

6. Improving Your Concentration

How long and how deep you can concentrate on a single subject is very important. You should be capable of doing that for a longer period than the average person if you want to be mentally stronger. Do not give in to distractions when you are focusing on something. Think about its breadth and depth. Consider all the variables present and you will be able to make the right choice.

7. Understanding Over Cramming

Many people will choose to cram over understanding because it is the shorter route. Yes, it could be shorter but it reduces your mental strength. A mentally stronger person can explain a new concept in their words as they understood it. Students who understand their teachers instead of cramming what they are taught are mentally strong. Make an effort to understand new things even if it is in small parts. The mind can never be full. You can only be tired but you can resume from where you paused it.

8. Keep The Company of Mentally Gifted People

Other people are mentally gifted. They understand new concepts the moment they are taught. Their analysis of everything is excellent and you can hardly find a fault with their thinking patterns. When you hang out with them, you will be able to study their thinking and approach.

You can borrow a few skills from their prowess. Knowledge, like foolishness, is contagious. Beware of your company.

9. Embrace Challenges

Mental strength can increase or decrease. It is dependent on one major factor – challenges. Do not run away from challenges. Face them head-on. The same challenge will not come to you twice and it will leave you better than how it found you. This does not mean you should go looking for trouble. Only handle whatever comes your way. Have an open mind that the challenge you are facing is a lesson in preparation for your next step in life.

10. Meet New People

Making new friends is not entirely a bad idea. Strangers can turn out to be best friends and even family! Your mind should be exposed to how different people run their things and their different approaches towards life. New people offer new experiences. These will strengthen your mind and approach to diversity.

Conclusion

The mind is like a muscle. Do not be afraid of committing mistakes. They offer a correction point of getting it right the next time. Practicing these ten ways will leave you mentally stronger.

Chapter 9:

8 Things Confident People Don't Do

True confidence is very different from egotistical swagger. When people believe in themselves and their abilities without bravado, there are certain things they simply don't do.

1. They Don't Make Excuses

If there's one trait confident people have in spades, it's self-efficacy -- the belief that they can make things happen. It's about having an internal locus of control rather than an external one. That's why you won't hear confident people blaming traffic for making them late or an unfair boss for their failure to get a promotion. Confident people don't make excuses, because they believe they're in control of their own lives.

2. They Don't Quit

Confident people don't give up the first time something goes wrong. They see both problems and failures as obstacles to overcome rather than impenetrable barriers to success. That doesn't mean, however, that they keep trying the same thing over and over. One of the first things confident people do when something goes wrong is to figure out why it went wrong and how they can prevent it the next time.

3. They Don't Wait for Permission To Act

Confident people don't need somebody to tell them what to do or when to do it. They don't waste time asking themselves questions like "Can I?" or "Should I?" If they ask themselves anything, it's "Why wouldn't I?" Whether it's running a meeting when the chairperson doesn't show up or going the extra mile to solve a customer's problem, it doesn't even occur to them to wait for somebody else to take care of it. They see what needs to be done, and they do it.

4. They Don't Seek Attention

People are turned off by those who are desperate for attention. Confident people know that being yourself is much more effective than trying to prove that you're important. People catch on to your attitude quickly and are more attracted to the right attitude than what, or how many, people you know. Confident people always seem to bring the right attitude. Confident people are masters of attention diffusion. When they're receiving attention for an accomplishment, they quickly shift the focus to all the people who worked hard to help get them there. They don't crave approval or praise because they draw their self-worth from within.

5. They Don't Need Constant Praise

Have you ever been around somebody who constantly needs to hear how great he or she is? Confident people don't do that. It goes back to that internal locus of control. They don't think that their success is dependent on other people's approval, and they understand that no matter how well they perform, there's always going to be somebody out there offering nothing but criticism. Confident people also know that the kind of confidence that's dependent on praise from other people isn't really confidence at all; it's narcissism.

6. They Don't Put Things Off

Why do people procrastinate? Sometimes it's simply because they're lazy. A lot of times, though, it's because they're afraid -- that is, afraid of change, failure or maybe even success. Confident people don't put things off. Because they believe in themselves and expect that their actions will lead them closer to their goals, they don't sit around waiting for the right time or the perfect circumstances. They know that today is the only time that matters. If they think it's not the right time, they make it the right time.

7. They Don't Pass Judgment.

Confident people don't pass judgment on others because they know that everyone has something to offer, and they don't need to take other people down a notch in order to feel good about themselves. Comparing yourself to other people is limiting. Confident people don't waste time sizing people up and worrying about whether or not they measure up to everyone they meet.

8. They Don't Avoid Conflict

Confident people don't see conflict as something to be avoided at all costs; they see it as something to manage effectively. They don't go along to get along, even when that means having uncomfortable conversations or making unpleasant decisions. They know that conflict is part of life and that they can't avoid it without cheating themselves out of the good stuff, too.

Embracing the behaviours of confident people is a great way to increase your odds for success, which, in turn, will lead to more confidence. The science is clear; now you just have to decide to act on it.

Chapter 10:

Improving Your Sleeping Habits

Sleeping habits are an important part of growth. It is sad how most people have degraded sleep and it has turned out to be a measure of laziness. If you truly want to know the importance of sleep, deprive yourself of it for a few days and watch how your body will respond.

The importance of sleep cannot be over-emphasized. Have you noticed how fresh and strong you feel after waking up from a long and satisfying sleep? It is not the short naps and siestas during the day but the total rest that you get at night. You should constantly improve your sleeping habits. There are bad sleeping habits as well as good ones. Here is a whole list about them and how they can be remedied:

1. Sleeping Late

Pushing daytime tasks into the night will not make you perform any better. Sometimes you may find yourself sleeping late because you did not realize time flies as you were storytelling. This is not enough justification. The remedy to sleeping late is developing a sleep schedule with consistent times to go to bed and wake up. Healthy sleep should be at least 8 hours long and uninterrupted. Depending on what time you want to wake up, observe bedtime time.

2. Sleeping With Tight Clothes

Some people sleep in tight clothes at night. This is unhealthy because sleep is a time of rest, and your body should feel free. Comfort during sleep is important. The remedy to sleeping in tight clothes is having nightclothes – a night dress or pajamas. They are highly recommended because they are tailored to factor in comfort during sleep. Do not sleep in jeans or clothes that you had during the day.

3. Constantly Checking Your Phone When You Go To Bed

Most 'modern' people are guilty of this crime – addiction to mobile phones. They carry their phones when going to bed (which is okay) but misuse them in bed. The misuse is that they start checking their social media and browser feeds when it is bedtime. The remedy to this misuse of mobile phones and other electronics is putting them aside when going to bed. This is not enough. Switch your phone to silent mode or turn on do not disturb (DND). Continued phone notifications will interrupt your sleep.

4. Listening To Music As You Sleep

The habit of listening to music on your earphones or speaker when you have gone to bed is unhealthy. Music may soothe you into sleep at the beginning but it is a distraction that many people love. No matter how loveable it is, loud music will deprive you of sleep. The remedy to listening to music in bed is that you do not use your earphones and lower the volume when playing on the speaker. Soft music will make you fall asleep. You can also set the music to switch off after about one hour or so because you would have fallen asleep already.

5. Oversleeping

Sleeping is good but too much of it is unhealthy. Sleep must be regulated. You should neither go to bed late nor wake up late. Find a balance between the two and you shall optimize the importance of sleep. The remedy to oversleeping is setting an alarm. It will help you wake up early and as well as observe your sleeping schedule. Alarms are noisy and you should check-up with your roommate if they are comfortable with it (especially if it goes off early in the morning).

Conclusion

Sleep is important for your well-being. Great sleeping habits will make you sleep better and healthier. Observe the remedies to these five bad sleeping habits to be on the safe side.

Chapter 11:

8 Bad Habits That Make You Age Faster

According to a statistic given in an article in Globe Newswire, it's projected that by the year 2019, the global anti-aging market will be worth 191.7 billion dollars! Clearly, a lot of people are investing in products and procedures to help keep themselves looking young and beautiful. But, as with any disease or condition, prevention is always far better than the cure, and the same holds true for anti-aging. Unfortunately, there is no magic fountain of youth that will keep you young forever. But there are some particular habits and mistakes that, when avoided, can make you less likely to need anti-aging products and procedures. If you're a person who is concerned about an aging appearance, it's going to be important to avoid the things that make you age faster!

1. Processed Foods

Foods that have been highly processed and refined not only lack the nutrients needed by the body to support proper functioning, they typically also contain synthetic chemicals and other harmful ingredients that are detrimental to health. These processed foods cause faster tissue breakdown and other cellular damage that leads to faster aging. Additionally, when the nutrients that the bodily tissues need to function optimally are not optimally supplied, both the function and appearance of the skin and other organs can suffer.

2. Smoking

Smoking is a habit that not only wreaks havoc on your health but certainly speeds up the aging process. Even smoking one cigarette causes a huge amount of oxidative stress. This oxidative stress causes wear and tear on the body's cells, causing many issues such as aging, wrinkles, and other forms of degeneration.

3. Drug Abuse

Too much drug use of any kind causes internal stress on the body that again causes dysfunction, breakdown, and lack of optimal functioning. Depending on the drug, some can cause water loss, loss of healthy fat tissue, toxicity and more that can leave you looking older and frailer.

4. Lack Of Hydration

Being improperly hydrated, especially chronically, surprisingly can make you look more aged. Water is essential for so many roles in the body that without enough of it, the function of the body suffers, which both directly and indirectly, can lead to quicker aging. Water gives your skin the soft, plump, vibrant, moist look that indicates health and youthfulness. Additionally, it helps internally to flush out toxins that can cause acne, red eyes, bags under the eyes, puffiness, and other ailments that certainly don't scream youthfulness!

5. Not Getting Enough Sleep

Getting insufficient sleep is a major way to age yourself quite quickly! A chronic lack of sleep causes the body to shut down. Your eyes become bloodshot and red, baggy eyes, wrinkled skin, low energy, and many other symptoms that make anyone look older than they are! Sleep is so important both for health and for beauty that there's even the common saying, "I need my beauty sleep!"

6. Stress

Being chronically stressed is another habit that wreaks havoc internally. Stress typically is also associated with other habits that hasten the aging process. When stressed, people tend to sleep more poorly, eat more poorly, take more medications and drugs, and other such things that disrupt health and advance aging. Chronic stress keeps stress hormones elevated in the bloodstream constantly, which can have negative effects on the complexion of your skin, both the coloration and wrinkles, and causes red eyes, and an overall slumped, broken down and aged function and appearance. Having these stress hormones elevated chronically can lead to a number of health problems, the least of which is wrinkles and aging!

7. Being Physically Inactive

Being inactive is a sure way of making your body look and feel older than it really is. Sedentary living typically causes you to have poor posture, become overweight, lethargic, and just plain droopy! Keeping your body moving and strong does a surprising amount for keeping you looking and feeling youthful from the inside out. Individuals who stay active as they get older typically age much better.

8. Prolonged Exposure to UV Rays

Getting too much exposure to UV rays, either from being out in the sun unprotected too much or from tanning bed use, really causes a lot of damage to the skin, leading to wrinkles, sunspots and other damage that makes you look old.

By consistently maintaining a wholesome, natural, active lifestyle, you'll automatically be on a better track for avoiding fast aging. Following a diet of fresh, natural foods, being active, managing stress, and getting proper sleep can do leaps and bounds for helping you stay youthful!

Chapter 12:

6 Steps to Get Out of Your Comfort Zone

The year 2020 and 2021 have made a drastic change in all our lives, which might have its effect forever. The conditions of last year and a half have made a certain lifestyle choice for everyone, without having a say in it for us.

This new lifestyle has been a bit overwhelming for some and some started feeling lucky. Most of us feel comfortable working from home, and taking online classes while others want to have some access to public places like parks and restaurants.

But the pandemic has affected everyone more than once. And now we are all getting used to this relatively new experience of doing everything from home. Getting up every day to the same routine and the same environment sometimes takes us way back on our physical and mental development and creativity.

So one must learn to leave the comfort zone and keep themselves proactive. Here are some ways anyone can become more productive and efficient.

Everyone is always getting ready to change but never changing.

1. Remember your Teenage Self

People often feel nostalgic remembering those days of carelessness when they were kids and so oblivious in that teenage. But, little do they take for inspiration or motivation from those times. When you feel down, or when you don't feel like having the energy for something, just consider your teenage self at that time.

If only you were a teenager now, you won't be feeling lethargic or less motivated. Rather you'd be pushing harder and harder every second to get the job done as quickly as possible. If you could do it back then, you still can! All you need is some perspective and a medium to compare to.

2. Delegate or Mentor someone

Have you ever needed to have someone who could provide you some guidance or help with a problem that you have had for some time?

I'm sure, you weren't always a self-made man or a woman. Somewhere along the way, there was someone who gave you the golden quote that changed you consciously or subconsciously.

Now is the time for you to do the same for someone else. You could be a teacher, a speaker, or even a mentor who doesn't have any favors to ask in return. Once you get the real taste of soothing someone else's pain, you won't hesitate the next time.

This feeling of righteousness creates a chain reaction that always pushes you to get up and do good for anyone who could need you.

3. Volunteer in groups

The work of volunteering may seem pointless or philanthropic. But the purpose for you to do it should be the respect that you might get, but the stride to get up on your feet and help others to be better off.

Volunteering for flood victims, earthquake affected, or the starving people of deserts and alpines can help you understand the better purpose of your existence. This keeps the engine of life running.

4. Try New Things for a Change

Remember the time in Pre-school when your teachers got you to try drawing, singing, acting, sculpting, sketching, and costume parties. Those weren't some childish approaches to keep you engaged, but a planned system to get your real talents and skills to come out.

We are never too old to learn something new. Our passions are unlimited just as our dreams are. We only need a push to keep discovering the new horizons of our creative selves.

New things lead to new people who lead to new places which might lead to new possibilities. This is the circle of life and life is ironic enough to rarely repeat the same thing again.

You never know which stone might lead you to a gold mine. So never stop discovering and experiencing because this is what makes us the supreme being.

5. Push Your Physical Limits

This may sound cliched, but it always is the most important point of them all. You can never get out of your comfort zone, till you see the world through the hard glass.

The world is always softer on one side, but the image on the other side is far from reality. You can't expect to get paid equally to the person who works 12 hours a day in a large office of hundreds of employees. Only if you have the luxury of being the boss of the office.

You must push yourself to search for opportunities at every corner. Life has always more and better to offer at each stop, you just have to choose a stop.

6. Face Your Fears Once and For All

People seem to have a list of Dos and Dont's. The latter part is mostly because of a fear or a vacant thought that it might lead to failure for several reasons.

You need a "Do it all" behavior in life to have an optimistic approach to everything that comes in your way.

What is the biggest most horrible thing that can happen if you do any one of these things on your list? You need to have a clear vision of the possible worst outcome.

If you have a clear image of what you might lose, now must try to go for that thing and remove your fear once and for all. Unless you have something as important as your life to lose, you have nothing to fear from anything.

No one can force you to directly go skydiving if you are scared of heights. But you can start with baby steps, and then, maybe, later on in life you dare to take a leap of faith.

"Life is a rainbow, you might like one color and hate the other. But that doesn't make it ugly, only less tempting".

All you need is to be patient and content with what you have today, here, right now. But, you should never stop aiming for more. And you certainly shouldn't regret it if you can't have or don't have it now.

People try to find their week spots and frown upon those moments of hard luck. What they don't realize is, that the time they wasted crying for what is in the past, could have been well spent for a far better future they could cherish for generations to come.

Chapter 13:

6 Routine Building Strategies

Creating a positive everyday life is an investment in yourself and a way to do your best for the rest of the world. It also offers additional benefits such as structuring, building the habit of moving forward, and creating the momentum to keep going when you feel powerless to act. Following a daily routine can help you set priorities, limit procrastination, track goals, and be healthier. As Tynan, author of Superhuman by Habit, puts it, this reduces your reliance on your will and motives because a habit is "an action you take consistently with little or no effort or thought".

Feel free to try a new habit and see how it works for you. If they give you energy and inspiration, keep going... If not, keep trying new things until you find one that works. The key is to help you maximize yourself on every level possible by creating regular, consistent daily patterns that will take you where you want to go in life. Now let's move on to a few things you can do in your everyday life to achieve higher mental levels (i.e. more extraordinary brain power and clarity!).

1. Get Positive: Start The Day With A Mantra.

According to the Mayo Clinic, thinking positively can help you manage stress and improve health. "Today will be the best day!"

Every day, as soon as you get out of bed, you should start saying these simple sentences (out loud). And yes, say to yourself in the morning after a night so short, or when you wake up with the weight of the world on your shoulders. Why? These six words lifted the mood for days to come. It's not the events that make your day good or bad, and it's your reaction to them. As Jim Rohn said, "You rule the day, or the day rules you."

You want to put your heart into good condition immediately. Because if you don't, you will try to tell yourself the wrong thing... But with positive thinking, you can overcome it. Ben Franklin asked himself every morning: What good can I do today?

Choose a phrase or question that resonates with you. It can be as simple as saying "thank you" out loud with a smile and acknowledging that you have a gift the next day.

2. Be Proactive: Don't Check Your Email First!

Do you check your email or social media accounts as soon as you wake up in the morning? Then start your day reactively rather than proactive. As Jocelyn K. Gley writes in her book Manage Your DaytoDay, "The problem with this approach is that it means spending most of your day on someone else's priorities."

For example, if you receive an email requesting work-related documents, you may need to provide them immediately, even if you plan to do sideline marketing. Or you open Facebook and see one of your friends is in crisis, and that can become your focus and prevent you from focusing on your problem or concern. Start your day by focusing on yourself. Then you will be in a much better position to help others and achieve more throughout the day.

3. Mentally Prepare: Visualize Your Success

Some of the best athletes in the world use visualization to prepare themselves to excel in their sports mentally. Close your eyes and imagine that you are the best and the best. Visualize your best results to place yourself in a shining situation. Include as much detail as possible in your visualizations by using all your senses and making your "training" more powerful.

4. Read A Book (Even if it's just a page)

Reading books has many scientific benefits. According to Emory University research, reading increases your intelligence, boosts your mental abilities (for up to five days), and may even enhance your capacity to empathize with others. Reading has also been shown to be more than half the risk of getting Alzheimer's... All of this helps to put your mind at ease simultaneously!

5. Make Yourself Accountable: Enlist A Partner or Mentor

Make a list of three people you trust and admire. Talk to each of these people and discuss exactly what you want to achieve. After the conversation, decide who will be responsible for the specific milestone you want to achieve.

6. Reward Yourself

If you consistently fall into the routine, reward yourself with something fun. For example, if your goal is to learn how to clean up a mess every night before bed, reward yourself with new slippers to enjoy in a clean home.

A healthy routine allows you to maintain the highest possible level of work in the three dimensions of existence: mind, body and spirit. It would help if you had it to get better. It would be best if you had this to keep looking at opportunities and seeing problems as "situations". In short, I need you so that you can be free.

Chapter 14:

8 Best Things to Do in Your Free Time

If you have a lot of free time, the best way to use it is to relax, have fun, de-stress after a stressful day, or spend time with a loved one. But if you only have a small portion - say 5 or 10 minutes - you don't have time for exciting stuff. So what do you do in your free time? Take these small chunks of time to make the most of them. Everyone works differently, so making the best use of your free time depends on you, your work style, and what's on your to-do list. But it's handy to have a list like this so you can quickly figure out how to spend that spare time working right away without thinking. Use the following checklist to get ideas for what you can do in the short term.

1. Reading Files

Clip articles from magazines, print out good articles or reports to read later, and keep them in a folder labelled "Reading File". Take it with you wherever you go, and whenever you have some spare time, you can remove items from your reading file. Keep a reading file on your computer (or in your bookmarks) for a quick read at your desk (or on the road if you have a laptop).

2. Clear Out Inbox

A meeting in 5 minutes? Use it to empty your physical or electronic inbox. If you have a lot of things in your inbox, you will have to work quickly, and you may not get everything done; but reducing your stack can be a big help. And having an empty inbox is a great feeling.

3. Phone Calls

Keep a list of the phone calls you need to make and the phone number, and take it with you wherever you go. Whether you're at your desk or on the go, you can remove a few calls from your list in no time.

4. Make Money

It's my favourite effective use of free time. I have a list of articles to write, and when I have a few minutes to spare, I will write half a paper quickly. If you have 5-10 free time a day, you can earn a decent side income. Figure out how you can leverage your freelance skills and prepare work you can get done quickly - break it down into chunks, so the pieces can be done in time short.

5. File

No one likes to do that. If you're on your game, you'll sort things out at once, so they don't pile up on top of each other. But if you've just been through a hectic period, you probably have many documents or files lying around. Or maybe you have a large stack of papers to file. Cut that number down with every bit of spare time you have, and you'll be on the Nirvana leaderboards soon.

6. Reading

Reading is a lifelong skill, and successful people never stop reading new books. Whether fiction or nonfiction, books help you better understand your world. They introduce you to new characters, environments, cultures, philosophies, and ideas and can even help you learn new skills (at least if you read nonfiction). Likewise, reading regularly helps build your vocabulary and semantic understanding, giving you better communication skills and what to do for small talk during difficult business meetings. Handle that.

7. Volunteer

No matter how or where you do it, volunteering benefits you and your community. Whether you're helping clean up a highway, working at a soup kitchen or mentoring a group of young professionals, your time will help you improve the communities around you in the long run. Successful professionals recognize the importance of giving back to the community and feeling happier. Volunteering is also a valuable networking experience, introducing you to others who, in one way or another, can help you advance in your career.

8. Spend Time with Friends And Family

Your job is not everything. Focusing too much on your career is self-destructive, which seems counterintuitive. Suppose you want to be successful in life. In that case, you need to prioritize your relationships with friends and family members. No matter how quickly you want to succeed and climb the corporate ladder, you can't neglect your friends and family to do it.

Conclusion

If you don't spend your free time like this, that doesn't mean you don't have a chance of success. However, by adopting some of these strategies, you can extend your network to levels that improve your skills, thinking, and opportunities for success in the workplace. When you start incorporating some of these into your off-duty routines, you may be surprised at the results.

Chapter 15:

Ten Ways to Make This Your Best Year

Not Business As Usual.

"Happy new year!" This was on everyone's lips at the beginning of the year. We wished each other well and we were full of expectations about what this year will bring to our tables.

What is so unique in this year that was missing in the previous one? Only one thing. Your age. It is the only thing that is in constant motion.

Having new year resolutions helps a lot. If you did not achieve your last year's, this too shall be unachieved. You can take that to the bank. You have to change your tactic if you want to make this your best year ever.

Here are ten ways you can achieve this:

1. Set Realistic Goals

You know your limits and what you are capable of. Your target should lie within those ranges. Do not overstretch yourself beyond your limits. You may not achieve much.

It is okay to have high dreams but take one step at a time if you want to maximize your potential. Unrealistic goals will instill worry in you and in this state, you really cannot do much.

2. Rest But Do Not Quit

It is not okay to quit on the ambitions you have for this new year.

Resting to rejuvenate your strength and you will recover from any setback you have suffered. This new year shall be your best ever if you learn to rest.

3. Consider A Self-Care Routine

Self-care is a very important routine. It will make you celebrate yourself more and be proud of who you are.

You need to be in the best form ever as you pursue your goals. Cheer yourself on and fall in love more with yourself this year.

4. Benchmark With Successful People

Successful people have a wealth of experience in whatever it is they do. First, identify what spikes your interest and the people successful in that field.

Learn from them what makes them stand out and implement the same in your projects. You will definitely have the same results as them.

5. Spend Time With Your Family

Family is the basic and most valuable unit a person can have. Despite all your busy schedules, spare some time for your family. They are the backbone of your success.

The more you spend time with people who value you, the more you also get to appreciate yourself. Do not waste any opportunity to unite with your family.

6. Follow Your Passion

Follow your passion at all costs for therein lies your success. If you have a passion for something, you invest your energy and resources in it. You also become more knowledgeable about it.

Do not follow other people for the sake of it. Be unique in your own way and you shall be rewarded for it.

7. Do Not Procrastinate

When you settle on doing something, do not postpone its actualization. Better yet, when a worthy idea comes into your mind, write it down in a notebook before you forget.

Thereafter, plan on how you can implement the idea. There is stiff competition in every industry. While you postpone your idea, another person elsewhere will implement it.

8. Consult Widely

Accept that you do not have a monopoly on ideas. Consult with more experienced people than you. They will advise you accordingly on how you can go about new ideas.

Wide consultation will give you the perspective of many people. You can thereafter sieve through the advice you have been given and act on the best one.

9. Go For Health Check-Ups Periodically

Health is wealth. You should pay attention to your health. Do not wait to go to the hospital at the last minute. Routine health check-ups are good because some diseases can be diagnosed on time, and you can get treatment.

Of what use is all the wealth you will accumulate if will not be healthy to enjoy it?

10. Set Up a Workout Routine

A workout routine is important for a healthy lifestyle. Enroll for gym sessions nearby and start working out today. It is not always about burning calories but staying fit and healthy.

Exercises will also improve your mental health. You will be stress-free as you follow up on your goals.

Start a new beginning today to make this your best year.

Chapter 16:

How To Cultivate a Wealth Mind-set

The euphemism for a "wealth mindset" dictates your energy to your finances. You don't have to be a millionaire to think and make decisions like one, but once you cultivate a wealth mindset, you're positing yourself for a win in your financial life. A wealth mindset is more about making the most of the money you have. Self-help gurus equate it to spending less, investing wisely, and figuring more ways to increase your financial standing.

The reward for strengthening a wealth mindset is massive. After hearing phrases like "money doesn't grow on trees," you can use an upgrade. Even if your goal isn't to amass a six-figure fortune, you can use these techniques to expand your financial security and abundance beyond your current status.

Here is how to cultivate a wealth mindset.

1. Consider Shrinking Your Debts First

One thing is for sure; you can't start accumulating wealth with outstanding debts hanging over your head. Pay off your debts first before you even do something else. Whatever steps you take to settle debts, be sure that your mental space will be in a better position to cultivate wealth mindset once you've done this.

2. Classify Your Ideal Fortune

This is not the classic generalization of a luxury home, steering wheel, or designer clothing. You want to go beyond the typical notion and create an outline of your desired lifestyle, professional work life, and mindset. This causes you to develop wealthy thinking and subsequently a wealth behavior. Understand that a mind is a powerful tool such that cultivating a broke behavior leads to a broke lifestyle and vice versa.

3. Refrain Using A Scarcity Mindset

Pessimism is one way to describe how a scarce mindset works. If you find yourself in a mental space where you are content to live "paycheck to paycheck," it's possible that you've developed a scarce mindset concerning money. This is defeatist thinking, and you'll find yourself constantly focusing on not having enough. Replace it with abundant thinking, which shifts your focus to see no limits to what you can achieve. That is because abundance thinking enables you to realize that there will be enough to meet or satisfy your goals no matter your financial situation.

4. Money Need A Criteria

From a practical standpoint, budgeting or having a financial plan make complete sense. The structure of this initiative is premised on the idea that your money requires direction and a plan to match your financial goals. Failing to make plans for your money will land you in a stagnant financial standing. You'll find yourself stuck in a cycle that always leads you to undesirable outcomes in your financial life. And once you've become accustomed to it, your mind will never consider other options.

5. Redefine That Making Money Is Simple from the Usual Assumption

Redefining your mind to believe that making money can be an easy journey is difficult. This is because everyone's mind is geared to believing that making a notable figure requires hard and grueling work. However, the more you fuel your mindset to see how simple this can exist in your real world, the more you'll be able to incorporate it into your practical life. Working on your wealth mindset necessitates removing old beliefs and replacing them with new ones.

6. Bypass People Lacking Ambition

The famous saying that an individual is the average of the five or few people they spend most of the time with cannot be taken lightly. People with a limited wealth mindset can stink you up with their lethal condition of complacency, leaving you glued in that levelled thinking. In order to maximize your desire to become wealthy, surround or acquaint yourself with those who have succeeded in creating wealth. This includes putting yourself in a position to absorb their knowledge and insight on cultivating your opportunities and start developing a wealth mindset.

7. Transform Your Financial Script

Negative wealth narratives can have dire effects on your financial state because what you think influences how you feel. Such negating narratives are capable of influencing the way you act, or make decisions and, ultimately, impacting on your end results. Consider substituting them with optimistic scripts that helpfully structure your financial life.

Conclusion

Cultivating a wealth mindset necessitates not only considering the above techniques, but also putting them into action. The more practice you put in, the simpler it'll become. Examine how you might be sabotaging yourself even as you diligently plan for your financial prospects and lay a new foundation for yourself.

Chapter 17:

The Battle Against Anxiety and Depression

The Loop of Life

We cannot help to be worried about this or that. Solving one problem gives birth to another complex one. This is the cycle we have to deal with. You may think that enough money can solve your problems. Once you have it, another one pops up.

Power too cannot solve your problems. It can only facilitate so much and after that you are alone. Ask those in power how much they crave privacy. Their lives are in constant public scrutiny. Consider the British monarch. The movement of members of the royal family is under constant watch. Even their private lives literally involve the whole world.

This is how our lives are in a loop. If you do not watch out, anxiety and depression will be your daily dose. They can never be fully eliminated but can be kept under control.

Be The Master.

The master is the one in charge at all times. When he does not have things under control, he ceases being the master. Similarly, take charge of your life. Control what is within your reach and let not exterior factors affect your lifestyle. This is how you can be in charge:

1. Do Not Succumb to Peer Pressure

Do not compare your lives with your peers and feel inferior to them. Your destinies are different as is your personality.

Social media has not made things any better. Almost everything is about competition. Everyone wants fame and success. It is astonishing the lengths that people can go for social media clout. When they fail to match the fake competition, depression sets in.

You are unique in your own way even if you do not belong to the 'class' of your peers. Do not compare yourself with anyone.

2. Understand Time and Seasons

Everyone has their destined time and season to shine. Do not be anxious about anything. Find comfort that your time for glory has not yet arrived. In due time, the world shall see you shine.

You may be worried that time is not on your side. Your colleagues could have their own businesses yet you have none. They could also be married while you are hardly in any serious relationship.

All such thoughts of comparison are uncalled for. Your time has not yet come. Trust in destiny as you work your way up the ladder of life. Cheer them and be happy for their success. Do not wallow in your pity.

3. Find A Hobby

A hobby is something that you love. You can do it for hours without getting fed up. It could be singing, writing, swimming, playing soccer, or cooking. Identify your hobby and spend as much time as possible doing it.

Your hobby will capture your time and attention. You will be occupied having fun and will worry less about things you cannot control. Hobbies are powerful drivers of motivation too. They can help you rediscover your joy and open a new chapter.

4. Find A Support Partner

You need a support partner in your battle against anxiety. Someone you will pour your heart to when you have no one to turn to. Depression can make you lose your senses. Someone needs to be there to help you restore your sanity.

A support partner can be a parent, spouse, or best friend. They should be understanding and preferably someone you can completely trust with your deepest secrets. You should keep nothing away from them.

Their help does not make you any weaker. Instead, you are forming a strong team against a common enemy – depression.

5. Seek Medical Help

The good news is that it is never too late to seek medical attention even after it has badly affected you. Something can be done about it.

The earlier you seek treatment, the better your chances of coming out of it safely.

You shall eventually prevail against anxiety and depression.

Chapter 18:

Health Anxiety for Men

Anxiety is a normal stress response. However, it can become harmful when it becomes difficult to control and influence your daily life. Anxiety disorders affect nearly 1 in 5 adults in the United States. Women are more than twice as likely as men to develop an anxiety disorder during their lifetime. Anxiety disorders are often treated with counselling, medications, or a combination of the two. Some men also find yoga or meditation to help with anxiety disorders.

Anxiety is a feeling of fret, nervousness, or fear about an event or situation. This is a normal stress response. This will help you pay attention in challenging situations at work, study harder for an exam, or focus on an important speech. It will help you deal with it in general. However, if the anxiety interferes with your daily life, fear of everyday activities that are not threatening, such as taking a bus or talking to a coworker, may make the anxiety go away. Anxiety can also be a sudden terrorist attack without a threat.

From an early age, boys are more likely to suffer from anxiety disorders than girls. In fact, by the age of six, girls are diagnosed with an anxiety disorder. This difference persists through adolescence and adulthood when twice as many men as women suffer from anxiety disorders. Boys were six times more likely to develop a generalized anxiety disorder.

Girls had higher levels of OCD before puberty. Men were more likely to have panic disorder, GAD, agoraphobia, and post-traumatic stress disorder. Men are twice as likely to have phobias as men. There are minor gender differences in social anxiety and obsessive-compulsive disorder.

Types Of Anxiety Disorders:

1. Generalized Anxiety Disorder

People with GAD worry too much about everyday health, money, work, and family problems. With GAD, your mind often goes to the worst-case scenario, even when you have little or no reason to worry. Men with GAD can worry about getting through the day. They may have muscle tension and other stress-related physical symptoms, such as trouble sleeping or an upset stomach. Sometimes anxiety prevents people with GAD from performing everyday tasks. Men with GAD have a higher risk of depression and other anxiety disorders than women with GAD. They are also more likely to have a family history of depression.

2. Panic Disorder

Panic disorder is twice as common in men as in men. People with panic disorder suddenly feel fear when there is no real danger. Panic attacks can cause feelings of unrealism, fear of impending doom, or fear of losing control. Fear of physical symptoms that one cannot explain is also a sign of panic disorder. People with panic attacks sometimes think they have a heart attack, lose consciousness, or die.

3. Social Phobia

Social phobia, also known as social anxiety disorder, is diagnosed when people are very anxious and shy in everyday social situations. People with social phobia are afraid of being viewed and judged by others. They can panic easily and often experience panic attacks.

4. Obsessive-Compulsive Disorder (OCD)

People with obsessive-compulsive disorder have unwanted thoughts (obsessions) or behaviours (compulsions) that cause anxiety. They may keep checking the oven or iron or repeat the same procedure to control the stress that these thoughts cause. Often, consciousness eventually comes to prevent a person.

Treatment:

1. Psychotherapy

The most common treatment for health problems is psychotherapy, specifically cognitive behavioural therapy (CBT). CBT can be very effective in treating health problems because it teaches you skills that will help you cope with your disability. CBT can participate as an individual or as a group. Some of the benefits of CBT include:

- Identifies your health concerns and beliefs.
- Explore other ways to change your mind and see how your body feels.
- Raise awareness of how your worries affect you and your behaviour and react differently to body sensations and symptoms.
- Learn to better deal with anxiety and stress.
- Learn to stop avoiding situations and actions because of your bodily sensations.
- You are avoiding physical examinations for signs of illness and seeking confirmation that you are consistently healthy.
- Improve your skills at home, at work or school, on social media and with others.
- Check for other mental health conditions, such as depression or bipolar disorder.

Other forms of psychotherapy are also sometimes used to treat health problems. This may include behavioural stress management and exposure therapy. If your symptoms are severe, your doctor may recommend medications along with other treatments.

2. Medication

If psychotherapy alone improves health problems, this is usually all used to treat your condition. However, some people do not respond to psychotherapy. If this applies to you, your doctor can recommend a drug. Antidepressants such as Selective Serotonin Reuptake Inhibitors

(SSRIs) are often used for this condition. If you have a mood or anxiety disorder in addition to anxiety, drugs used to treat these conditions may help. Some medications for health problems have severe risks and side effects. It is important to discuss treatment options with your doctor carefully.

Chapter 19:

Seven Signs You are Depressed and How to Overcome It

The Difference is Not the Same

The modern world has many challenges compared to how it was before. Life is getting complex by the day and the building up of these activities affects your mental health in one way or the other. The American Psychiatric Association defines depression as a common and serious medical illness that affects how you feel, think, and act. It is more of a mood disorder than physical sickness. Depression is indiscriminate of your social status. You can hardly tame it without external help.

Laziness on the other hand is nowhere near a medical condition. It is a lifestyle choice that many people call selective participation. Laziness is majorly characterized by idling. You can do something, yet you will not do it because you just don't feel like it. It is a disappointing habit that claws back on the gains you may have made. Depression makes you lose interest in doing things that you once enjoyed. You oscillate between bad moods and total disinterest even in how you relate with people. It also directly affects your functionality both at work and at home. It is important to draw a line between depression and laziness or else you will have a lifetime of difficulty overcoming either or both of them.

Here are seven signs that you are depressed and how to overcome them:

1. Deep Feelings of Sadness and Hopelessness

Do you feel an emptiness within you? This is the first tell tale sign that depression is knocking at your doorstep. Depression creates a void in your heart and you get detached from the rest of the world. You always want to be alone and wallow in your pity.

Seek Motivation

Part of the reason you feel this way is because you are demotivated. Mingle with extremely motivated people with a high self-drive in what they do. Positivity, just like negativity, is infectious. You will snap out of depression and live a motivated life.

2. Feelings of Guilt and Shame

Depression will make you feel unloved, guilty about things you have no control over, and shameful for reasons you cannot explain. You want to do something yet you don't because guilt and shame are eating you up. A lazy person does not think of getting things done. But a depressed person will make an effort but some invisible force will hold them back.

Improve Your Confidence and Self-esteem.

Do not blame yourself for past failures. Something new and exciting has started in your life. Some of the ways you can build your confidence are:

- Talk to the person in the mirror.
- Have a positive mindset.
- Don't be ashamed to talk to others.
- Set realistic goals.
- Invest in yourself.

Believe in yourself and you shall eventually overcome depression.

3. Sleep Disorders

Do you hardly get enough sleep? Or do you oversleep once you finally get some sleep? You are probably depressed about something. It could be that you can quickly point it out or you could have no idea what it is. The lack of sleep (insomnia) and oversleeping are signs that you are depressed.

Plan To Have Adequate Rest and Do It

It is not enough to plan to have enough sleep. You will be alert the following day when you have enough sleep the night before. Sleep depriviation will make you less effective at work and reduce your general performance. The cause of insomnia could be endless thoughts and once you regulate your sleeping habits, you have equally overcome depression.

4. Thoughts of Self-harm and Suicide

Depression makes you see that the end of the road has come. It makes you lose hope completely and think of an easier way out. None of them can cure what you are going through. This is a fatal phase that can make you ruin what has taken you years of struggle to build.

Seek Professional Help

Therapy works even for those who seem to be very much depressed. A professional can guide you out of this unpleasant and unfortunate phase of life. It can be too much to do it alone but with the help of someone else, it gets easier.

5. Slowed Thinking and Actions

A person who is depressed has slowed thinking which could be so much unlike them. This is because their minds are occupied elsewhere trying to solve something else. Slowed thinking and actions can cost you an arm and a leg. This is how expensive depression can be if not addressed timely.

Come To The Present

Come to the present and do not drift too far away. Being alert and alive to your surroundings is an important tool to fight depression. Engage in something that will constantly make your mind think about the present and not let you wallow in your pity. Play around with your puzzle block, your prayer chain, and anything that will make you be in the present.

6. Trouble Concentrating

If you are having problems concentrating on what you do then you could probably be depressed. Your mind cannot settle on what it is that you want to do because there is something else bothering you. Sometimes it becomes noticeable and you become absent-minded.

Confide and Trust In Someone

Curing depression sometimes only requires you to open up. Talk to someone you trust about what is bothering you. This will remove the burden on your heart and you can concentrate fully on what you do. Do you know what they say? A problem shared is a problem half solved.

7. Angry Outbursts and Frustration Over Small Matters

You stop being rational when you are depressed. Depression makes you magnify small wrongs when someone else commits them. If you have been having this behavior lately, you have a reason to be concerned. Frequent anger outbursts are an emotional outlet to hide depression. They are hardly genuine.

Address The Root Cause

The chief reason for such frustration is not that something has gone wrong but is depression. You can overcome it by looking beyond veiled excuses. Addressing the real reason for your behavior change goes a long way to overcoming depression.

Depression is the new pandemic. Although it may seem difficult or impossible, you can overcome it when you make a sober decision to do so. Accepting that you are depressed is not easy but is the first step toward regaining your momentum.

Chapter 20:

How To Deal With Stress

Stress is an inevitable part of everyone's life, and it's no secret that stress wears on your emotions and wreaks havoc on your physical health. Men face unique challenges and have unique needs for stress management. The circumstances are that as a woman, you are juggling many responsibilities that you barely have time to manage stress; such that when you find yourself in a stressful situation, you handle it in an unhealthy way like overeating, drinking alcohol, or just laying around.

While it's almost impossible to do away with all the stress in your life, you can manage the situation and improve your health. A personalized care plan that includes time to recover and self-care can help you handle stress and motivate you to make healthier lifestyle choices. So how can you manage stress in your life?

Here is how to deal with stress.

1. Classify the Problem

First, classify the stressors in stressful situations rationally and how you responded to them. Keep a record of the events that caused your stress, including who was involved, the physical setting, and how you reacted. Taking notes can help you identify patterns in your stressors and reactions to them, allowing you to develop a stress management strategy.

2. Make Use of Mantras

Think of a mantra, and in this particular case, there are two effective ones; "I'm sure I can do it" or "That's not going to work for me." The former sentiment reminds you that you're capable of completing the task at hand. While the latter assures you that you are not always required to. Give your all to the things worth your time and effort, and let the rest go. You don't always have a choice, but when you do, it's okay to say no if saying yes will push you beyond your healthy limits.

3. Choose Your Battles

You don't always control external stressors, but you can practice restraint when it comes to internal stressors; that is the expectations you place on yourself. There's no reason trying to be all things to everyone and then feeling like a failure if you don't get to do everything.

4. Get Enough Sleep

A good night's sleep gives you a competitive advantage. Sleep is a form of self-care and one of the most effective ways to meet your physical, mental, and emotional needs. Giving up sleep is the same as giving up fuel. You get refuelled after a good night's sleep, which helps you manage and reduce stress.

5. Figure a Way To Grow in the Challenge

Stress can cause you to think in a limited, pessimistic manner. However, this does not have to be the case all the time. Find your happy medium and calm those overwhelming or stressful thoughts. You'll probably become tolerant of stressors once you find a different approaching perspective.

6. Engage in a Physical Exercise

Exercising for your mental health doesn't have to be as rigorous as training for physical fitness. Almost any kind of regular exercise will get you there. Whatever type of exercise you choose, rest assured that it will lower stress hormones produced by your body while enhancing your mood-endorphins.

7. Chill Out a Bit

Unless you're in a life-or-death situation, a twenty-minute break won't hurt. Instead, take some time off and engage in things you enjoy doing. You can read, have a latte with a friend, or even enjoy your favorite show. Taking your mind off your problems reset your mind such that you return to them with a fresh perspective.

8. Get Organised

Nothing beats stress than being prepared and organised. It gives you a sense of control you may never imagine. Nothing exacerbates your stress like that piled-up paperwork, or a cluttered kitchen, or a backlog of emails. Set some time aside to address the issue or seek assistance.

9. Talk to Someone

Sometimes your problems become bigger when you keep everything to yourself. Get out, and talk to someone, be it a friend, or more so seeking professional help. Talking things out enables you to find solutions to your problems, thus triggering stress management.

Conclusion

Societal expectations are that a man must multitask and do everything expected of a "typical man" to earn a place or be valued. Resist and do things on your own terms because once you conform to such expectations, you're opening an avenue for mental health issues. Don't let this strenuous and frazzled world get the best of you.

Chapter 21:

Ten Traits of A Truly Honest Person

Who is honest?

But who is truly an honest person? The answer to this question is stingy because of the uncomfortable true answers. An honest man or woman is one who NEVER compromises on the truth. They are unapologetically truthful despite the possible harsh consequences that might fall on them. Quite a few people are honest with themselves and others. The truth is a bitter pill to swallow and not everyone dares to take it. Many people are becoming dishonest for a variety of reasons, yet they manage to disguise themselves as masters of the truth. Honesty begins when one opens to speak the truth without omitting anything. Telling the truth selectively in versions that would favor you also amounts to dishonesty. The scope of honesty is wide, and this makes it difficult for someone to easily identify a truly honest person.

The character of an honest person.

1. They Are Ever Consistent

Honest people are ever consistent. They will repeat exactly what they told you the last time you asked them the same question. They never contradict themselves about what they said. This is the first test you can give to someone if you want to judge their character. If they fail it, there's no second chance.

2. They Have No Hidden Motive

There is always a motive behind all our actions. Honest people have motives too. However, one thing with them is that they are always clear-headed and have nothing hidden in their sleeves. They will always reveal the motive for their actions and even if they do not, you can easily read it from them. Their intentions are always pure and well-timed.

3. They Are Fair in the Administration of Justice

Honest people are always level-headed and make the soberest decisions. They have no favoritism and would say the truth as it is. You will notice their fairness when they are pronouncing themselves on matters in which they could be possibly conflicted. They always stand for the truth regardless of who it may hurt.

4. They Are Dedicated To Their Work

Honest people take their work seriously and dedicate their time and effort toward it. Their work matters a lot to them and always give honest input into it as per the agreement they agreed with the employer. Other people may give divided loyalty and effort to their work, but honest people are truthful even when there is no one supervising them.

5. They Are Content in What They Do

Most people are hardly content with their work. They will always look for a way to have extra gain even if it involves a little bit of dishonesty.

Honest people never defraud anyone. They believe in making an honest living even if it means little gain. Their values and principles come first before anything else.

6. Their Words and Actions Are In Sync

A dishonest person would say one thing and mean another. There is never a match between their speech and actions. Matter of fact, if you want to prove their dishonesty, simply investigate the relationship between what they say and what they do. In extreme cases, they say things only for public relations and have no intention of following it up.

7. They Keep Promises

Promises are willing commitments that one makes without any influence whatsoever. Honest people do not make promises for the sake of it. They mean what they say and live up to their word. Like all upright people, they believe that one's word is their bond. Honesty begins by following what you willingly commit before you fulfill obligations that tie you.

8. They Are Principled

Honest people live by their life principle – truthfulness among others. They cannot compromise their beliefs over anything. All their actions and thoughts are firmly anchored on their principles. Their fidelity to keep them makes being honest with other people easier.

9. They Are Quick To Admit Their Mistakes

Not everyone admits when they are at fault. Unlike them, honest people are quick to admit their mistakes and make deliberate efforts to make amendments. They are honest with themselves and others not to blame someone else for something they are liable for. They confess their mistake even when nobody saw them. Honesty begins with themselves and then proceeds to other people.

10. They Are Straightforward and Upfront

Honest people have no time to beat around the bush. They believe the truth will remain unchanged no matter how twisted you try to make it look. What makes them lovable is how they hit the nail on the head and speak truth to power. They stand out from everyone else who shies away from the truth.

Conclusion

Handling honest people requires courage because if you are not honest, they may put you in your rightful place. Use these ten traits as a guideline to identify a truly honest person from your pool of many friends.

Chapter 22:

Five Signs You Cannot Trust Someone

The Universal Currency.

Trust is the universal currency that people trade on. Business dealings, employment opportunities, and relationships are all based on trust. A lot of things go wrong when this foundation is shaky. Trust is a deal-breaker on many fronts. It is not a gift. It takes a lot of investment to earn it from someone. It could take months or years to prove your trustworthiness and the same can be lost within minutes. Trust directly impacts your reputation. It is difficult to turn things around when people have a history of mistrusting you. Mistrust begins in a very small way and gradually reaches a non-negotiable point where nobody wants anything to do with you. It would help to know early signals of mistrust in people. Here are five major ones:

1. Unkept Promises

This is the first sign that you cannot trust someone. Your word should always be your bond if you want to win the trust o other people. You would rather not promise something you are not sure you can fulfill than give false hopes or assurances to other people. If a person cannot follow up on something that they willfully promised, how can they be trusted with other responsibilities? Understandably, sometimes things get beyond our control. However, you a series of unkept promises is a red flag that someone is not trustworthy.

2. A Bad History of Shortchanging Other People

Your relationship with other people speaks a lot about the kind of person you are. If someone has constantly been untrustworthy, how can they be trusted in new relationships? It could be true that someone has changed for the best, but they have to prove themselves to be worthy of your trust because of their bad history. Statistics have never lied. They are an accurate representation of reality. You can easily predict where someone is headed if they have been untrustworthy in nine out of ten situations. You cannot trust them.

3. Constantly Defending Their Trustworthiness

There is no need to go on a rampage swearing and doing all manner of things to defend your trustworthiness if you are indeed innocent. The truth shall eventually vindicate you. Somebody who is always defensive has something to hide. A trustworthy person has nothing to defend himself against because his record speaks for him. Consider it like a court case. The accused has the burden of proving their innocence because of the incriminating evidence against them. The innocent have no reason to prove themselves as so because there is nothing against them. Beware of people who are often defensive because there is often more than what meets the eye.

4. Constantly Shifting Blames To Other People

People who always blame others for their failures are not to be trusted. It cannot always be the fault of other people. You have a role to play in your success or failure. Someone who always finds another person to blame cannot be trusted with anything because they can withdraw from your agreement and shift the blame to you. It is a sign of lack of accountability on their part and you should have nothing to do with them until they put their house in order first. If they cannot be accountable for what is already is in their plate, how can you trust them with more responsibilities?

5. Zero Track Record of Honesty

There is a reason for a scorecard in job evaluation. It is a measure of your performance in the capacity you hold. A good scorecard means that you were once trusted with responsibilities that you carried out to perfection. It also means that you were a good manager of resources that were entrusted to you. This is a good history and a sign that you can be trusted with more. Do you know of the biblical story of the workers and their talents? The one with one talent hid it in the ground and returned it to his master as it was. Those with five and ten talents invested in them and got a profit. Their master trusted them with more. Likewise, you can trust people with a proven track record of trustworthiness.

Conclusion

The next step after identifying an untrustworthy person is to know how to live with them or avoid them completely because they are a liability to your cause. They may put a blemish on your noble mission.

Chapter 23:

Morning Book Routine for Men

Would you like to embrace reading into your morning routine? Studies show that reading a few pages in the morning enhances your memory, improves your mental health, increases your creativity and productivity, and sets a positive tone for the day ahead. The idea of owning your A.M habits isn't always easy, but the benefits you reap from it are astounding. So just set aside a few minutes for a book morning routine that will enrich your mind and teach you novel things.

Just like vigorous physical exercises in the morning will prepare you to be more physically resilient during the day, positive mental training in the form of inspirational reading will prepare you for a mentally fit day. When you're busy, it's certainly a challenge to read, but it isn't unlikely. How are you going to pull it off?

Here is a morning book routine for women.

1. Set Your Daily Goal

It's essential to be as specific as possible when setting your morning book routine goal. Consider your reading expectations and what you hope to accomplish so that you can devise an effective strategy to get you there. For instance, do you want to read your books in a month or a few weeks? Which writer or genre piques your interest the most? It's always a good idea to develop a habit of consistency and to establish a morning book routine that promotes your growth.

2. Make Time in Your Schedule

Reading daily can be difficult, but instead of putting it off and telling yourself that you'll do it some other time, you should be intentional or proactive. Setting an intention to read motivates you to do so and it will assist you in reaching your goal. Making time in your schedule to read every morning is the simplest way to ensure that you do so. Put your energy in it just as how you take completing the tasks on your to-do list. When you are time-barred from your book routine, treat it with the same reverence as everything else.

3. Eliminate Potential Distractions

A worthwhile book routine means getting rid of any potential distractions that might cause your time set for reading a good book. Put your cell on a silent mode, or unplug any devices that might compromise the silence, or whatever it takes to enjoy reading a good book. Making time to read in the morning and sticking to it also serves your discipline when scheduling time for essential things like rest days or spending time with loved ones. It also strengthens your time management techniques.

4. Read What Intrigues You

You might be tempted to finish that classic or read a novel that your friends are raving about. However, if you don't enjoy what you're reading, you may delude into believing that reading is the issue rather than the content. It's never a concern disliking a specific genre or a book. What matters is whether your morning book interests you or makes you happy, and more importantly, whether it stimulates growth or positivity in your daily endeavors.

5. Choose Your Genre

The main idea is to create a morning book routine with genres or authors who interest you. You can also look for those books with positive reviews from other readers, the ones that fit or suit your personality. Fuelling and keeping your book routine going is more likely when you get into a genre that promotes your growth and supports those positive vibes.

6. Get Into Niche Books

Consider reading books and topics that you love within your industry or line of business. This gives us a better understanding of your line of business and a competitive advantage. Digging deeper into niche topics or areas you're interested in can help you cater to more people and create innovative ideas that take you to the next level.

7. Learn To Embrace Change

Because the world is an unpredictable place, there will always be mornings that force you beyond your control, throw you off guard, and disrupt your tried-and-true morning routine. To be forewarned is to be forearmed. If you're prepared for disruption, you'll be in a much better position to go with the flow and keep your eye on the prize. You can't, of course, deviate from or abandon your routine.

Conclusion

With just a life-changing book morning routine, you can truly shine. All it takes to keep it consistent and exciting is reading what you enjoy and changing up content once the boredom kicks in. The essentiality of reading daily is associated with an active and healthy mind.

Chapter 24:

How To Stop Being Lazy

How can I stop laziness?" The answer may not be as cut and dry as you'd expect. While some people may be more prone to being lazy than others, even highly productive people can find it challenging to get things done sometimes.

Here are some tips to help you get rid of laziness and get a grasp on your productivity.

Make Your Goals Manageable: Setting unrealistic goals and taking on too much can lead to burnout. While not an actual clinical diagnosis, the symptoms of burnout are recognized by medical professionals. Job burnout can cause exhaustion, loss of interest and motivation, and a longing to escape. Avoid overloading by setting smaller, attainable goals that will get you where you want to be without overwhelming you along the way.

Don't Expect Yourself To Be Perfect: Perfectionism is on the rise and it's taking a psychological toll. One 2017 study that looked at college students between 1989 and 2016 found an increase in perfectionism over the years. Researchers noted "young people [are] now facing more competitive environments, more unrealistic expectations, and more anxious and controlling parents than generations before." This rise in perfectionism is causing people to be overly critical of themselves and others. It's also led to an increase in depression and anxiety. Another smaller study of college students concluded that expecting perfection was related to avoidant coping, which causes you to avoid dealing with stressors.

Use Positive Instead of Negative Self-talk: Negative self-talk can derail your efforts to get things done in every aspect of your life. Telling yourself that you're a lazy person is a form of negative self-talk. You can stop your negative internal voice by practicing positive self-talk. Instead of saying, "There's no way I can get this done," say, "I'll give it my all to make it happen."

Create A Plan of Action: Planning how you will get something done can make it easier to get there. Be realistic about how much time, effort, and other factors are needed to meet your goal and create an action plan. Having a plan will provide direction and confidence that can help even if you hit a hurdle along the way.

Use Your Strengths: Take a moment to think about what your strengths are when setting goals or gearing up to tackle a task. Try to apply them to different aspects of a task to help you get things done. Research has shown that focusing on strengths increases productivity, positive feelings, and engagement in work.

Recognize Your Accomplishments Along the Way: Patting yourself on the back for a job well done can help motivate you to keep going. Consider writing down all of your accomplishments along the way in everything you do, whether at work or home. It's a great way to boost your confidence and positivity, and fuel you to carry on.

Ask For Help: Many people believe that asking for help is a sign of weakness. But not asking for help could be setting you up for failure. A 2018 study found that people who don't ask co-workers for help were more likely to be dissatisfied in their jobs and had lower levels of job performance. They were also perceived less favourably by their employers. Asking for help improves your chances of success and helps you connect with others who can encourage and motivate you.

Avoid Distraction: We all have our favourite distractions we turn to when we're just not feeling like doing a task — whether it's scrolling through social media or playing with a pet. Find ways to make your distractions less accessible. This can mean finding a quiet place to work, like the library or an empty room, or using an app to block sites that you scroll mindlessly when you should be on task.

Reward Yourself: Getting a job done is a reward in itself, but some people are driven by external rewards. Focus on what you'll gain from getting something done, like getting closer to a promotion, or reward yourself for a job well done. Celebrate the end of a big project with a night out or invite friends over for drink after a day of cleaning.

CPSIA information can be obtained
at www.ICGtesting.com
Printed in the USA
LVHW081346110822
725656LV00010B/173